Once Upon a Tinder

Dare to Love Again

By
Dr Ann Donnelly

Copyright © 2021 Dr Ann Donnelly

All rights reserved.

ISBN: 978-1-7330955-7-0

Copyright Notice: No part of this publication may be reproduced or transmitted in any form or by any means, mechanical or electronic, including photocopying and recording, printing and reselling, or by any information storage and retrieval system, without permission in writing from the publisher. You ARE NOT AUTHORISED to give, sell or share the contents of this publication. If you have received this e-book from a source other than kdp.amazon.com you have been given a pirate copy. Please help to fight this crime by sending notice of the incident to thelovedoctor@onceuponatinder.com

LEGAL DISCLAIMER

The entire content of Once Upon a Tinder, must be considered as exclusively informative and cannot in any way be understood as a substitute, alternative or supplementary of professional opinions or medical consultations, nor refer to specific individual cases, for which we invite you to consult your own attending physician and / or recognized specialists. The contents of Once Upon a Tinder are for informational purposes only and should not be intended to diagnose, prevent or treat any ailment or disease. The author of this work declines any responsibility for any consequences deriving from a use of its contents other than merely informative.

Nothing contained in this work constitutes or intends to constitute a suggestion of any nature. As the user of Once Upon a Tinder, if you feel the need for advice in relation to any topic, you are invited to contact a qualified professional in the specific field.

If the user of Once Upon a Tinder suspects or is aware of having or having had or being exposed to problems, disturbances and / or physical or psychological illnesses and in any case, must rely on appropriate medical treatment recommended by a professional of their own trust

Despite the scrupulous care used in the preparation of Once Upon a Tinder, drawn up with the utmost accuracy and diligence, it is not possible to ensure that the information contained within it is free from errors, omissions or inaccuracies.

Dr. Ann Donnelly disclaims any liability, direct and indirect, towards readers, regarding inaccuracies, errors, omissions, damages, deriving from the aforementioned contents.

The author of Once Upon a Tinder cannot guarantee the users of the book to obtain the same results of personal character growth, psychological, motivational, physical or any other nature or denomination on a par with as set out in this work.

Within Once Upon a Tinder the ideas of consultants and experts are cited and hosted which in an absolutely free form, not constituting what they affirmed an opinion of a professional or similar nature, offered their contribution for information purposes only, without any presumption or willingness to place oneself above the recognized traditional medical system. It is at the free discretion of the user of Once Upon a Tinder and its absolute responsibility for any willingness to follow or replicate some of the advice proposed therein or to contact other competent personnel, according to your own beliefs, knowledge, habits and wills.

Everything included within Once Upon a Tinder must always be understood as the subjective opinion of the author, given that these considerations can also run counter to the precepts of knowledge taught in universities and / or in the scientific world and therefore are there considered as simple expressions or controversies of a personal and in any case non-professional nature, having to make exclusive reference to/and reliance solely on traditional and recognized fields of knowledge.

Published by: Dr. Ann Donnelly

Attention: The content of this text is inspired by real facts although it does not represent the absolute reality of the events narrated therein. The work represents the fruit of the artist's creativity. The names, places and certain circumstances narrated have been deliberately altered in order to respect privacy. The purpose of the work is intended to provide a point of view of the narrator, who can legitimately depart from other perspectives of subjects hypothetically involved.

WHAT PEOPLE SAY

This book has so many things. An amazing mix between romance and teaching knowledge, as well as a reminder of the great energy a man and a woman can create! Making it ok to be a woman. The vulnerability and stories are what a lot of women around the world have gone through and are going through.

It's defiantly from the heart! It's nice to read something pure. No agenda, just real life!

Divina Franca Lanyon President of the Modern Mystery School, International Instructor, Member of the counsel of twelve women.

As someone who is going through divorce and who has gone through a challenging marriage, putting myself back in the game was frightening for me. Yet as the pages turned, the joy of getting to know and love myself has sunk in, with useful information on how to take the steps.

I started blossoming under the loving, writing hands of Dr. Ann Donnelly, and everything in my life shifted to reflect that.

I wholeheartedly and highly recommend this book to any woman who wants to feel sexy, desired and loved again.

Mirav Tarkka,
5 times best selling author, Speaker and coach.

Dr. Ann is one of the most courageous & gifted guides of our time, daring to step outside the safety net into the unknown field of dating in your 50's.

This little book is simple, practical, and yet profound. Packed with gems of wisdom, love, information and knowledge. It will have you laughing out loud and shedding a tear or two along the way.

Dr. Ann captures very well the delicate dance between valuing yourself & allowing your potential partner the same privilege.

This book is witness to a tender presence to Self. The stories beautifully illustrate what is really achievable when you know, honour & acknowledge that presence and beauty within. A must read for all those who "Dare to Love Again".

Rose Reel Psychotherapist and Holistic Practitioner
M.I.A.C.P., M.B.A.C.P., C.B.P.

All of us go through ups and downs in our professional and our personal life. The key to a happy and successful life is learning from every situation and finding the pieces that serve us best while leaving the rest.

Dr. Ann Donnelly's book motivates the readers to look at life with joy and happiness in the little moments and to live life to the fullest. The most important aspect of any relationship is self love and *Once Upon a Tinder i*s the perfect guide that will help you fall in love with the most amazing person in your life- YOURSELF. And once you inculcate this love for yourself, you will find love in your relationship with others.

This book will take you on a beautiful journey, it will make you laugh, it will make you cry but most importantly it will help you understand the most important human emotion and feeling-LOVE.

Parul Agrawal
Author, TEDx Speaker,
Business Growth Strategist

When I put down "Once Upon a Tinder" I felt hope. Hope for all those women who suddenly find themselves on their own, after a long relationship, stranded in the unknown.

Hope that life is far from over, that yes you can start dating again and have fun doing it. Once Upon a Tinder is funny but at the same time it's honest and vulnerable, which is what makes it such a good read.

Not to mention the handy tips for those who want to venture into online dating Apps!

A book, which people will read more than once!

Heidi De Love, bestselling editor and author

What an incredible story about a middle-aged woman looking for a new relationship after divorce. However, the dating scene has changed beyond recognition since she got married twenty years ago. I love the true picture of Dr. Ann's main character exploring her sexuality and using modern dating Apps to find her new life. I highly recommend this exceptional book to women of all ages, who are ready to move forward towards love, intimacy and exciting life adventures!

Martina Wojtylova Opava, Wellbeing and Energy coach, mentor, best-selling author, founder of the Endowment fund helping abandoned newborns, wife and mother of 2

DEDICATION

To all the women and all the men looking for love
Let's make this world a more loving place ♡

CONTENTS

Letter To The Reader — xv
Chapter 1: How it all Started — 1
Chapter 2: A Little Know How — 6
Chapter 3: My First Date — 12
Chapter 4: Self Care First — 17
Chapter 5: A Second Go — 21
Chapter 6: Good Boundaries — 26
Chapter 7: A surprise! — 31
Chapter 8: The Chemistry Behind Falling for Someone — 35
Chapter 9: The Three Gregs. Greg Number 1 — 40
Chapter 10: Getting to know you. Getting to know all about you. — 42
Chapter 11: The Three Gregs. Greg Number 2 — 46
Chapter 12: What's Love Got To Do With It? — 48
Chapter 13: The Three Gregs. Greg Number 3 — 54

Chapter 14: Love, Lust and Everything
                 In Between 59
Chapter 15: Changes 63
Chapter 16: The Widower 67
Chapter 17: Mindset 71
Chapter 18: The Rock Star 76
Chapter 19: Polarity Between The Sexes 82
Chapter 20: Growing Bolder 87
Chapter 21: YOU, HIM, HER, THE
                 ENTIRE UNIVERSE 91
Chapter 22: In Summary: Tips To
                 Take Away 94
Acknowledgements and Gratitude 101
About the Author 106

Letter To The Reader

There are probably an infinite number of reasons why you might be drawn to take time out of your life to read this book. Whatever the reason, I thank you.

As a student of life, a Goddess, creating my own unique world I have always been fascinated by people, and their stories. I have noticed how their quality of life is coloured by the nature of their closest relationships.

One relationship, we often overlook, is the most intimate relationship of all, the one we have with ourselves. This is the foundation to everything.

What do we really desire? What are we willing to negotiate? Where do our boundaries lay? What is non-negotiable?

One thing we can be sure of is that all relationships are here to teach us, and the depths we are willing to go to, will proportionately reward us with our deepest desires.

Furthermore, life teaches us. As we grow we gather experiences and form opinions. Those opinions change according to our perceptions at any given time. In order to get the most out of life we need to delve deeper, beyond mere opinion.

Unfortunately, the vast majority of life is experienced through the subconscious mind. Here, we store unresolved issues from the past. They come up time and time again, to be recognised and healed. Our relationships, especially our closest, are where it will play out the most. Imagine if we cleared out the subconscious mind? Imagine if we could be more present in the current moment. Imagine what our relationships would look like if we did not project our past onto them, thus dictating the same outcomes over and over.

It takes a brave soul to really look inwardly. In the beginning, we may not like what we see. It is through true examination, with the discipline it takes to keep going, that we reach the goal of tender compassion towards oneself. Only then can we authentically extend compassion to others.

This book invites you to take a glimpse at the way we relate to each other as men and women, how this is magnified through the looking glass of dating Apps, and how to navigate the conundrums these inevitably generate.

I've been through the maze and learned from the experiences. Men and women have regularly asked me for advice and so I wrote this book, generated a website, and fostered engagement on social media to tease out the learning points and create better understanding and more LOVE between men and women.

If you would like to connect please feel free to email me, at **thelovedoctor@onceuponatinder.com** or check out my website **onceuponatinder.com**.

If you would like to know more about the tools that I have studied to help me navigate life I'd be delighted to share more information with you. There is a Path towards self-mastery, which helps us become the best version of ourselves and it's here for everyone to explore.

Personally, I'd like to take this opportunity to wish you every JOY as you create your own adventure into LOVE. Remember, stay safe, choose wisely, trust your gut and honour yourself.

With my LOVE always,
Di Ann ♡

Chapter 1
How it all Started

I moved out of our marital home 5 years after my husband asked me for a divorce. Why FIVE YEARS? Well, we were married for fourteen years when he dropped the bombshell. I spent the next three years trying to understand and mend what had gone wrong. In our case, the relationship was in tatters and he could not bring his heart and soul back to me. When we realised it was fully over I moved out and made tentative steps towards life on my own.

There are multiple ways of separating, divorcing and letting go. This was our way, albeit rather lengthy and a tad clumsy. It taught me one thing though. 'When it's over, it's over. Don't look back'. And so, on to the next chapters of my life.

I looked at many properties. Where we lived had been pretty much my dream home, so it took time to find somewhere that would nurture me while

I rebuilt my life. I found a little row of cottages by the water. I knew I wanted to live in one so I put a beautiful card through each letterbox saying, 'Hi! I love your home! If you are planning to sell or rent in the coming months please do not hesitate to contact me'. Two months later I got a call and I moved into the perfect spot.

I should set the scene.

I was brought up as an Irish Catholic. Divorce was a huge No-No and something that I never anticipated.

If you are an Irish Catholic too, I will gently warn you, I plan to talk about sex throughout this book! For the faint hearted, stop here. Of course, for some of you the explorations will seem very innocent. For others it will be down right, promiscuous but the coming chapters tease out what it may take to rediscover your mind, your body and your soul after the break up of your most significant relationship.

In addition, when you arrive at the doorway of your late 40's and early 50's there is a threshold. It is a rite of passage and I never anticipated just how juicy mine would be!

In the coming pages you will find fictional stories with underlying threads of truth. They are a collage of my observations of this wonderful world, its wild inhabitants, and my personal experiences.

On the topic of sex, even though I knew male anatomy really well before I got married, and I knew what to do with it in order for both parties to experience ultimate pleasure, I was a virgin when I got married at the tender age of twenty-nine!

At the age of forty-eight I had never had 'coitus' (I'm a fan of the TV show The Big Bang Theory and this noun will be used throughout this book) with any other man, other than my husband.

Please don't get me wrong. I had multiple relationships growing up, each fulfilling, loving and sexually satisfying without penetrative sex. If I'm honest, parts of me missed that.

Knowing each other well enough to trust each other to the tantalizing effects of each other's kisses, hugs, eyes, tongues, fingertips, hands, bodies without penetration? Phew! I feel another novel coming on!

Please note gentlemen, for most of us ladies; it is easier for us to climax from external clitoral stimulation!

The truth is I hadn't had any intimacy for over FIVE YEARS! AND I wasn't ready to trust anyone EVER AGAIN.

Or so I thought.

I will let you in on one little secret. Days after my husband asked me for a divorce I feared lots of things, but one thing that stood out for me was the very irrational idea that I might never have sex with another human being again!

So I called a couple, both dear friends of mine, and asked them to come on an adventure with me to Ann Summers (A British retailer specialising in sex toys and lingerie). I spent over £200 that day on all sorts of gadgets, vibrators, lubes, underwear, and books and on my return home, I started to play.

I desired pleasure with an intensity that is hard to explain. I guess I thought it would numb out the devastation for a while. **Interestingly, from that moment forward any city I travelled to in the world, I made it one of my priorities to visit at least one sex shop and treat myself to a new toy.**

Did you know that Tokyo has a sex shop with 6 floors in it?

Truthfully, the art of pleasuring yourself is something that every human being really ought to be well versed in. It is surely one of the greatest gifts we have been given! Please don't waste it!

The stories around this adventure would fill another book but suffice to say, I know my own body very well.

I moved out and brought all my toys with me. It was January. It was bleak weather-wise with long nights and short spells of daylight. I felt a mixture of excitement, fear and a little loneliness but I was absolutely determined to start over. I filled my home with things that made me feel loved.

The furniture for my boudoir was French and ornate, very feminine. Each corner had art, music or flowers.

I bought my own pole for pole dancing and borrowed a ladder to ascend into the attic.

There I marked the struts to ensure I wasn't going to collapse my lovely ceiling under the strain of my body weight. My teacher came once weekly and slowly I found a connection to the art of tease again.

Still, it took my dear gay friend Bert and his partner Ernie to sit me down for THE talk.

Chapter 2
A Little Know How

'Things have changed since you last dated Ann'. 'The way to meet people now, is on online.'

They recounted story after story regarding the experiences of friends on various sites. Finally they recommended two Apps with a few words of caution.

'Bumble, a respectable bunch. Tinder, variable encounters'. They showed me how to download the Apps and they proceeded to set me up with profiles on both before I had time to say 'fiddlesticks'!

When you set up your personal profile choose a few photos. Be honest, up-to-date AND put in a little effort. This is the first impression you want to give! The App will link to one of your social media sites, often Facebook, to verify your identity. This will take things like your age and display it on your profile, unless you are prepared to pay a monthly fee to choose what you want to display and what you don't. Without paying, you can choose the age range you are happy to date.

I don't know what was on my mind initially, but I chose age 28 and upward! There were a surprising number of interested parties but we can explore that later!

If you use a paid option you can also choose things like the distance your App reaches around the world. This is useful if you travel and want to plan dates abroad. Something to consider though, the social norms around different Apps vary in different countries.

In Italy, for example, Tinder is pretty much exclusively a 'hook up' App, meaning its usually just about sex. So be aware what impressions you are giving unless it is all about sex for you and hey, then, it's a win-win situation. However, remember to always take recommended precautions in ensuring your own safety.

The rest of the information you display is totally up to you: job, education, where you are from and a little information about yourself. You can reveal as little or as much as you wish. You can be funny, serious or quirky; it's your choice. Try a few different photos, one at a social event shows you mix well and maybe one of you, engaging in a hobby.

Soon there were matches flooding in.

Swipe left if you don't want to meet them. Swipe right if you would consider meeting them. In the beginning I swiped right a lot!

It takes a little time to understand the process, to weigh up characters, to build your confidence in sifting through who is a good match for you. In the beginning you might feel a little 'desperate' to meet someone. Anyone!

We have all been there so don't be harsh on yourself!

When you swipe right, if he has seen your photo already and swiped right it will come up as a match and you have the option of starting a conversation.

On Bumble you have to be the first to chat otherwise the match will expire in 24hours. On Tinder either of you can start the conversation.

The wonderful thing about a dating App is that it's just an online conversation. No pressure. If it results in a date, great! If it doesn't, that's cool too!

So relax.

Take your time to get to know someone. You can gauge their politeness and authenticity by the flow of the conversation. Do not feel you have to give any personal information until you are ready to meet them.

Meanwhile, I'd like to suggest a few pointers. I

must explain that I am writing from a heterosexual woman's perspective but many of these tips could be used by anyone.

1) Photos

For the gentlemen reading this book. It's pretty obvious that many men don't take a lot of selfies. They commonly choose photos of social events and if they are into sports there can be multiple people in every photo so it's not always clear which one is actually you! That's a definite swipe left for me. It sends out the message that you want to hide. Believe me, we want to see you! Have at least one shot with only you in it, or crop one to reveal your identity.

2) Flesh

I'm in two minds about the amount of flesh I see in a photo. Some people genuinely work out and it's a big part of their life. They are proud of what they have achieved and rightly so. There is no harm in showing off their abs and who knows, it might be love at first sight. However, when it comes to porn pictures, I would say, 'RED FLAG LADIES'. Do not under any circumstances be tempted to see who is behind the pretty penis shots. Firstly it's unlikely to be his, and secondly if they are that up front about why they want to meet you is it really worth it? If that is what you want maybe it's different but honestly it could be sleaze all the way and I'm not sure you really want to put yourself in that position. You don't know ANYTHING about this person and you are your most valuable commodity. I suggest you DON'T RISK IT!

3) Then there are the 'no-smilers'.

If they look grumpy in the photos they wish to attract you with, it's not likely to get any better in the flesh. A person's personality is commonly written all over their face, unless they are having a bad day, but after all, these are the photos they are saying that first 'hi' with!

4) Is it all flash and no substance?

Pictures of expensive watches, cars, maybe a boat, his crotch and no face photo.... it actually happens... that's probably a player. Why would someone play all their money cards up front, unless they are having you on, or perhaps, they are just rather intolerable?

5) The Ex

Honestly, are you trying to attract a lady/gentleman by showing us a photo of your last date and you? Eeeeeew.

6) Boozy photos

If they have a glass in their hand in every shot, or it looks as if they are drunk in every shot, think twice.

It might be the only photos they have but seriously, do they have a day job?

AND ONE MORE. But, it's a goodie.

7) Wedding ring

One of my biggest turn offs and SERIOUSLY ladies/gentlemen!!!! A photo of someone wearing a wedding ring?

Use your discernment! Don't ignore your instincts.

Chapter 3
My First Date

I got chatting with this very good-looking guy in his early 30's. We exchanged a lot of funny messages and I was building up a picture in my mind.

He worked in finance and he lived 10 miles away so meeting was a real possibility and who knows? We might even like each other. Of course, Tinder back then was just a messaging service with no video content like you have now. Video was added as an antidote to the COVID-19 Pandemic, and the long periods where one couldn't meet new people.

So, was he as gorgeous as his photo and online persona suggested? I wanted to find out and there is something about that anticipation that just builds day after day when you fantasise a little about that first date.

We communicated every day for a few weeks. The conversation was mostly about our day, and the funny things that happened. Then, he brought up the topic of meeting each other. Although I liked the idea I have to admit I was nervous. You have to remember something here. I hadn't been on a first date for nearly twenty years!!

And this person was a lot younger than me. My outlook in life has always been very youthful. And as I was soon to learn, you can meet a very immature fifty year old and a very mature twenty-something year old. Age does not determine maturity!

We negotiated for an evening meet up. He asked me to choose the meeting place, as he wasn't as familiar with the area. I chose a coffee shop by the waterfront. It was early evening so it would be dark but this area was well lit with lots of people around and I had my backup! My lovely gay friends, Bert and Ernie, were on telephone standby if things were in anyway dodgy. An important tip!

I worked at the local hospital. I could feel my heart pounding as I left. Then a sudden thought popped into my head. I didn't know everything about this person. What if I worked up close to his aunt, or worse again his mother? I've generally never been someone who cared what other people think about me but I did torture myself for a good half hour until I down right told myself, it's only coffee. It's only coffee!

That shower after work, the preening, the blow dry and curling, the moisturising and makeup, the perfume and the choice of attire down to the height of my shoes was fun! Some Tinder profiles will include height. It's not a big deal for me at five foot six inches as that's comparable to most men but it might be for you. Let's say I put in a little effort. I had a light dinner as I was nervous and I always fill up quickly when I'm nervous.

I parked my car close by and walked to the cafe aware of every person I met. Could that possibly be him? My heart was pounding a little more forcefully in my chest as I sat down. There was a sense of relief when I knew the waiter. He is always so courteous and particularly attentive to me. I sat by the large waterfront window, facing the door. I was a few minutes early. I declined to order anything, saying I was waiting on someone.

Timing on a date is important. If someone is both enthusiastic and thoughtful they will be on time unless there has been a really good reason. In this case they will acknowledge their lateness with an apology and offer an explanation. Keeping someone waiting is generally rude in most cultures. If you are someone who is habitually late, set yourself a different time scale. Set alarms. Make an effort! I know! I was one of those people until **I met an incredibly successful**

gentleman who taught me a lot about etiquette and how to communicate your affection through attention to detail.

7.30pm came and went. A thought entered my head. What if he was already in the restaurant and watching my reaction? I sat up straight in the seat and looked around. There was no one bearing his resemblance. I ordered a decaffeinated mocha and checked my phone. No messages. At this stage we were still messaging each other on the Tinder messaging service. I waited.

The mocha was warm and chocolaty. People came and went. I watched carefully the faces of strangers walking by outside. The lights of the coffee shop lit up their countenance well enough for me to see if he was one of the many. Not a peep.

Half an hour went by and it was obvious he wasn't turning up. I called Ernie. I was a little choked up. My first Tinder meet-up hadn't turned up!!! 'Come round immediately Ann! I'll put the kettle on'!

If it weren't for my friends I'm not sure I would have stuck it out. That evening they wrapped me up in a big blanket and we plugged my phone into their enormous television. We opened up the Tinder App and looked at the profiles that presented themselves. Some were immediately 'swipe left'. Anything from a really grumpy photo, to someone completely outside my age bracket (which was still rather generous at that point), to rude comments, or porn photos, all swiped LEFT.

Then there were the 'swipe rights'. Photos where the person had made an effort, with profiles that appeared genuine and interesting. We had a giggle. Bert was very empathetic to all the gentlemen. Ernie was a little more cutting in his comments but between us all we had the most heart-warming belly laugh and although my ego was bruised…'what if he had turned up and decided to run away when he saw me?', my enthusiasm to give it another go was renewed.

Friends. Genuinely, what would we ever do without them?

I went back to his profile the following day. Still, no message. I wrote, 'I turned up. You didn't.' and I deleted his profile.

Chapter 4
Self Care First

On your 'desperate days' don't go against your instinct!!!

There may be days when you would do anything to feel the arms of a tall dark handsome stranger around you, however my lovely, YOU need to LOVE YOU FIRST.

You will hear this over and over again but how does this play out in your life?

What makes you feel like a Queen? Have you a personal list of things that make you feel wonderful and do you practice them regularly?

A salt bath or salt scrub in the shower. It is so cleansing for your body and your energy field.

Fresh flowers. At one point in my life when I was very low I saw a delicate bunch of pink roses in the local supermarket for a few pounds. I took them home and unwrapped them from the unsightly plastic wrapper. I took lots of empty glass jars from my cupboard and I cut each bud to fit a jar. Then I kissed each little bud and placed one in all the rooms of my home.

Each time I entered a room, I found that little reminder that I too, would one day, blossom again.

Remember, if you don't have someone to buy you flowers, go right out there and buy some for yourself and while you are at it, if you can, buy a second bunch. Once you have paid for them at the checkout, give one of the bunches to the stranger behind you in the queue. Everyone loves flowers and you will make someone's day! Little acts of kindness for others will lift you too!

Journal. For me, I like to write poetry. It helps me express what is inside.

Meditate. It will help you remain calmer and decrease the 'monkey mind' that criticises you when you need it least!

Skin care. Taking time to depilate, buff and moisturise! It makes me feel on top of the world.

Nail care. Toe nails need regular attention summer and winter and if your job allows, make sure your fingernails sparkle too.

Underwear. It might only be you who sees it but

that knowing will give you the confidence to walk a little taller and strut your stuff like you got it baby.

Time in nature. It's the most non-judgemental place on earth and filled with fresh air and feel good factors.

Exercise. Those endorphins will help you glow and a regular practice will make you strong and healthier.

Dance. Put on your favourite music and dance on your kitchen floor baby. Shake that booty.

Friends. A catch up, some time to share your innermost thoughts, to laugh and to cry with each other.

Massage. Whether you have someone in your life or not oils, fragrance and touch are an antidote to just about anything. I remember after my marriage broke up going for my first massage. Surprisingly it was a male masseuse. He was so kind as I was visibly upset. He had healing qualifications in Reiki and I remember being transported to a very healing space. It helped me relax so much.

Sleep. Make sure your bedroom is your boudoir. Make it a space for sleep, masturbation and sex, when sex is part of your life. Invest in toys. Experiment. You deserve to feel satisfied and to educate your lovers. Don't be shy. Every woman is different, so it's your job to play with yourself and find out what works for you. When you are ready, the lucky guy who comes into your life really ought to be interested in what works for you too. It's part of getting to know each other when you are ready as a couple to connect sexually.

Then, when you feel more content in yourself or you are continuing to work on feeling content, and you still feel a desire for companionship, that's the time to swipe right.

Chapter 5
A Second Go

My next Swipe Right struck gold. I still smile when I think of him. Thirty-two years old. An Italian radiographer based in a hospital, which was a forty minute, train journey away. I could tell his enthusiasm, as he was keen to meet right away. We made plans. He would travel to my city and we would have lunch together. We would meet on a Saturday morning. I hadn't actually heard his voice. We were still messaging on the Tinder App but things were moving much faster with him.

I remember how bright the sun shone that morning. I was excited. Despite the previous experience the human spirit always bounces back and I know **I was put on this planet to love men and maybe even inspire other women to do so too. The opposite sexes have spent way too long tearing each other down**.

Because he was traveling I wondered if we might end up back at my home. I had tidied and I made sure I had some fresh pasta in the fridge. There were a lot of questions running around in my mind. What is the etiquette around first dates and first kiss, first hand holding, first hug, first intimacy? But I decided to just see what happened.

When I arrived he was there before me. I recognised him immediately. The most incredible dark wave of hair, a few inches taller than me, the kindest brown eyes that never left me, so polite pulling out the chair so I could sit and as soon as he spoke, oh boy. That accent.

He was strongly built, not skinny. Dressed casual but really well. We sat opposite each other and looked into each other's eyes as we spoke.

He was from southern Italy. One of three boys, he was the middle child. Both his parents were still alive. He spoke affectionately about them. He had been living in Ireland for 10 months and here was the defining moment. He was planning to move to Manchester, home of his favourite football team, in three months time.

We looked at each other. We each ate a delicious lunch and then decided to walk around the ancient walls of the City. He had never done this before so it was my turn to speak about the history of the place.

It was chilly despite the bright sun. We walked close together. When we talked our faces, our lips were tantalisingly close and there was obvious attraction.

His enthusiasm was infectious! He got cold about half way round and we walked closer. He wasn't dressed fully for the bracing Irish wind on the walls that day. We decided to come back to my place. Normally, I wouldn't advise this on a first date with someone, before you really know more about them, but he lived a train journey away and it felt really natural to continue getting to know each other.

By the time we arrived at my home it was dinnertime. He loved his food and wanted to help in the kitchen, which was great! We cooked the fresh pasta with vegetables and created a salad with a tangy lemon dressing and lots of pepper. I'm vegetarian so there was no meat at the table. It didn't bother him even though I could tell he liked meat. The one thing that stood out that evening was this. He wanted to take the relationship slow.

I cannot tell you what a great relief this was to me. We kissed passionately and we fitted together so well. I could not wipe the smile off my face. He took a photo of me that evening. I was lighting the candles on my silver candelabra. I was smiling so big and looked so happy that I still have that photo.

I left him to the train late that evening after

many laughs, many kisses and just being affectionate. My heart was taken by his sincerity, openness and gentleness. He asked me why we hadn't connected before now, with only three months left in Ireland? I explained I was new to Tinder. We resolved to date each other for the time he had left and to enjoy that time together.

We really clicked. We spent a lot of time in nature, exploring the beauty of the beaches, the hills and the forests close by. We would eat out when he wanted meat and meet up with his Italian friends locally. They worked in Italian food businesses and would bring me little gifts of new preserves they were trying out. I found their love of family so heart-warming and it made me smile how protective he was of me. If someone was giving me a little too much attention he would step in and join the conversation to make sure everyone knew I was his girl. It wasn't intrusive, simply endearing. People would really look at us when we were out together. I looked younger in his presence. He was so mature for his age. Always taking care of his friends and his family.

I knew he hadn't had many lovers before me and he was nervous. He had been in love once before and she had broken his heart. We started with him exploring my body and what really turned me on. He loved to watch the changes that happened to me when I climaxed. I responded to him so easily.

When we were together we took the time to explore one another and that time was so precious. It gave each of us an understanding of the other. Neither of us presumed what would work for each other.

Our appreciation of time spent together was heightened by the fact that it was likely to be short. It was as if time slowed down. We saw each other twice weekly until it was time for him to leave.

That was tough. I could feel his growing desire for new adventures in a new city. I knew he would leave soon. It was his birthday just before he left. I bought him his favourite Milan football shirt. He cried.

We never saw each other again.

Chapter 6
Good Boundaries

If you are looking for a steady relationship and you are meeting people with that in mind, there are things that you never want to assume about the other person. Assumption is the enemy of truth and it's ok to be direct, as you want to meet someone who is not going to mess you around. However, feel your way with the timing of the following questions. Use your intuition and discernment.

If they are not looking for the same things as you, you will save yourself a lot of heartache. Remember overall there is time, don't listen to the stereotypical 'I need to be married with 2.5 kids by thirty! Pleeeeease.

If a relationship is what you are after, I suggest you have the answers clarified BEFORE you plan to be intimate.

1) Ask your date, What are you looking for?

Don't assume that you both want the same thing. The longer you wait to ask this, the more likely your potential mate will answer you in a way that will make you happy rather than tell you the truth. Also do you really know what you are looking for? Take time. Maybe you desire a selection of sexual encounters. Maybe you desire a longer term loving relationship. What do you really want?

2) Ask the following question. Are you in a relationship right now or would anyone be offended by the idea that we are meeting each other romantically?

Never take it for granted that the slate is clean when you meet someone for the first time. If you want an exclusive relationship then make sure your intended feels the same way! In the beginning, when you are meeting lots of potential dates this isn't as important, but, as you become more selective, ask.

3) Ask, Do you prefer monogamy? If so, what does monogamy mean to you?

If this is important to you, does it mean being both sexually and emotionally exclusive with one another?

This applies to you too. Make room for your 'someone special'.

4) Questions about their last relationship.

You may want to leave these questions until a few dates in, but it will have a bearing so don't leave it too long. How long ago was their last relationship. You want to be careful of investing in someone who is on the rebound.

How long was the relationship? Is your date a serial non-investing, short-term dater and are you just one in a long list?

Or, was their last relationship a long relationship? It is generally felt that it takes someone 50% of the time they spent in the relationship to get over it. It can of course be shorter if they are actively working on themselves and taking responsibility for their feelings.

You might also ask why it ended. Is your date putting all the blame on their ex or are they openly accepting of their part to play? Do they exhibit insight and growth as a person?

Or was it genuinely a horrendous situation in which case, do they have self-esteem issues? Why did they stay in a relationship that was not good for them?

You might consider asking, if you were to ask their ex why it ended, what would they say? This will help you understand their ability to take the desires of their partner into consideration. The answers to these questions will give you a fundamental insight into the amount of personal development your date may or may not have done.

5) Of course you want to know how they feel about you.

This is a reasonable question. It's not because you need validation, but you genuinely would like to know where this is going. You could say you enjoyed their company and you would like to know, based on their first impressions, what they think of you. If they are hesitating and not all in, maybe be cautious about how much you wish to invest going forward.

If things are not working out, it's ok! Note it as a learning experience. It has taught you more about what you are looking for.

STOP letting your thoughts eat you up inside. Instead, concentrate on creating the life of your dreams!

Take full responsibility for your thoughts, feelings, words and actions.

No one else, including your date, is making you feel a certain way.

Now they may be treating you in a way you don't like, and if you don't like it, you address it. If there is no change you can always call it a day.

Why am I making this sound so simple?

Because, it is. You are in the driving seat of your life. Use the steering wheel to navigate where you desire to be.

We complicate things because we don't like change.

We prefer to be comfortable or to accept 'less than' because it's easier than radically changing our lives.

But change is the nature of living.

There may be growing pains but it is worth it.

I will be honest, I didn't ask any of the above questions in the beginning, because I wasn't ready for a 'relationship'. I wanted to rediscover myself, my body and have some fun along the way!

Chapter 7
A surprise!

It took me a little while to feel the desire to go back to dating Apps again. I guess there was an instinctual self-preservation mechanism taking hold. Next time, however, I found myself on the other dating App. I found myself on Bumble.

I swiped Right on a gentleman with flaming red hair. He was tall, skinny, adventurous and living in Dublin. His family was sixty miles from me and he came up regularly to see them. He held great conversations online. He was bright, quirky and appeared confident.

He was thirty-three but had experienced the most unusual life. He had graduated in law and went straight into retail, fast taking on a managerial role. He was very successful, but really didn't enjoy it. He met a girl from Argentina and followed her there but she broke his heart after moving there to be with her. He found himself in a strange country with no prospects. But he had one thing, a gift with people.

He was in a bar chatting with strangers one day when he met the boss of a huge worldwide cooperation. He was offered a job right away. He never turned up because he just assumed the guy was being polite and speaking through his drink. When he received a call to ask where he was, he realised it was for real and after three years in Argentina he was able to return to Dublin and continue his work from there.

When he arrived in his Mercedes to collect me for dinner I invited him in while I put on my coat. He was visibly nervous and looked a little younger than his photo. We planned to go to my favourite restaurant. I took him by his hand and told him I really looked forward to getting to know him. He relaxed. When we arrived, the waiters, who knew me very well, and who always treated me like Royalty, showed us to our table.

They looked at me, then at him, then at me again. New date?

I smiled. We ordered. We chatted. We got to know each other better. We laughed together. He treated me so well.

On our return home we kissed. It was the gentlest of kisses. So tender and so soft.

The bedroom was our next stop. **Interestingly, he just wanted to satisfy me.** That was it, over and over and over again. It is hard to forget that night, for all the right reasons! Some memories are independent of the mind. They are stored in the body and this was one of them!

He had an ability to find my clitoris with his tongue and to not let it go. He wanted to play down there and I was not complaining. When he came up for air he would look into my eyes and smile. We would kiss and then, he just went back down and continued until we eventually fell asleep.

What actually made me even more surprised was our morning routine. A kiss that started on the lips, moved down to my nipples and oh boy he ended up between my legs again. **I was in ecstasy**!

The least I could do was cook breakfast.

He was most definitely a lean meat eater! My vegetarian cooked breakfast wasn't what he was used to but that was not going to deter him from coming back for more.

Our intimacy grew where 'coitus' became part of our togetherness and that was still very gentle and loving. We saw each other on and off for a long while until he moved to London where he took a high-flying job working in the financial sector. I would still occasionally hear from him out of the blue.

A text filled with very longing statements of how we were meant to be together.

He touched my heart, big time.

Such a beautiful soul.

Chapter 8
The Chemistry Behind Falling for Someone

Sometimes the whole process of falling for someone can feel like you are going insane. There are good chemical reasons for this.

Romantic love triggers primitive areas in the brain releasing a cocktail of chemicals leading to both physical and emotional responses.

Our hearts flutter, our cheeks flush, and our palms may feel sweaty while emotionally we get mixed feelings of passion and nervousness.

1. Dopamine, a chemical associated with pleasure, is triggered leading to the type of high we associate with drinking alcohol. Feeling high or drunk on love is not uncommon.

2. The magic of romantic love is further enhanced by the hormones oxytocin and vasopressin. Both are released during intimate contact where skin meets skin. Notably oxytocin is also released during breast-feeding which helps bonding between mum and baby, so it's not surprising that it deepens connection after intimacy. It also helps create a feeling of calm and relaxation. Vasopressin has also been associated with long term bonding.
3. Meanwhile, cortisol levels increase in response to any stressful thoughts like the uncertainty of the question 'does she/he like me?' This can lead to a lower serotonin level and subsequent overbearing thoughts akin to infatuation!
4. Interestingly, romantic love also deactivates a neuronal pathway responsible for negative emotions like fear and critical judgement. We may find ourselves overlooking obvious hindrances to long-term connection, like lack of compatibility. We are blinded by our infatuations. I always recommend taking a little time to get to know someone and listen to your friends. They can see without the 'rose coloured spectacles'.

As time moves on and love proves itself, emotional ups and downs ease and the influences of cortisol abate. This leads to more comfortable feelings. It's reassuring to know that studies have shown that dopamine activity in the brain can remain a factor in long-term relationships without the stressful cortisol response. Indeed those who lose intimacy can also re-trigger the oxytocin effect by endeavouring to physically reconnect.

Sex is an important connector in romantic relationships. If either of you are having difficulty it is important to talk openly with your partner and to seek help to recover intimacy whatever that looks like for both of you.

Regarding dating Apps, it's easy to become addicted to the Left/Right highs and lows. I recommend only two Apps maximum at a time. Pay for one and use the free option for the other. That way, you can explore the benefits of both.

If you feel it is becoming too much, give yourself a break for a week or two.

Keep your eyes peeled for the person who walks past you every day.

There are different ways of widening your circle without Apps but you have to put in effort and I appreciate this is more challenging in today's COVID-19 cautious world. But let's have a look at what is possible!

Firstly, you have your social circle and while this

may be larger for some than others you will perhaps have a friend who has an even wider circle of friends. Approach them and let them know you are looking for a relationship. Can they recommend anyone in their circle? They will know an array of possibilities.

Next join a group, which gives you the added benefit of self-improvement. It may involve spiritual improvement, health improvement or a class to improve your public speaking! People who are into self-improvement are generally good eggs so consider an online class to begin!

There are of course singles events, which have also moved online. So check those out!

The interesting thing about bars and clubs is, although they are fun places to hang out, you are less likely to meet a 'long-term' partner there. It does happen, but it's less likely. If you are looking for a quality person you may need to step outside your comfort zone.

If you plan to widen your social circle by taking up a new hobby, let your motivation be to create new friendships. In that way, there is no pressure, and closeness grows organically.

In these days of social distancing it's important to stay safe.

It does however give you more time to work on the self-care pieces that will give you the confidence you desire when we are able to meet again.

There is nothing wrong with taking it slow.

Meet lots of people.

Become comfortable with the 'happily ever after' not quite happening today.

Remember when you do find what you are looking for, there will be a new kind of work for you to engage in.

It's good to have your own life in order as much as possible.

Until then, it's simply a matter of NEXT!

Chapter 9
The Three Gregs. Greg Number 1

Sometimes a name will come up regularly and it's just an observation. Although three men may have the same name they have zero in common. There was this one Greg who was a police officer working in a very highly trained special branch. At least that is what he told me.

He had a very straight-laced profile but when he got talking he would send really naked photos of his athletic body. Truth be told, we had already established a rapport and it was challenging to delete such pretty pictures. This guy worked every inch of his body. I don't think there was a piece of fat anywhere and he did reveal all parts from memory!

The mistake you must not make is that someone like this is necessarily interested in developing a 'relationship' with you. Please. Don't put yourself through this. He will connect when he requires a little flirting, ranging from receiving your reaction to photos of his erect penis, to down right sexting. Sexting is where you both text back and forth things you would pleasurably enjoy if you were together. It may include pictures or not. I don't recommend sending identifiable photos of you. You never know where they will turn up and it's not worth the angst.

Interestingly we met once for a cuppa in Belfast. He was every inch as real as his photos. It was a brief meeting. He kept touching me the whole time. The conversation was all about what he would like to do with me. He made no secret of what he wanted and although I was intrigued something told me not to go there.

So I didn't.

Chapter 10
Getting to know you. Getting to know all about you.

By the time we reach a certain age we feel we have done it all, experienced it all (like a grown up teenager) but nothing could be further from the truth. We never stop learning. Life teaches us that. And one of the most intense learning grounds is within a relationship.

The most fundamental relationship we experience is the one we have with ourselves. Personal ideals and how real life lives up to those ideals can differ. Never stop dreaming, never stop planning and taking the action required to realise those dreams. This means we never stop growing. That is the true adventure of life and it has the added benefit of keeping you young!!!!

So whether it has worked out for you in the past or not, you have a choice whether to dip your toe back into the dating world again or not. You can take breaks. I did. However being the incurable romantic that I am, it was rarely long before I went back for more.

The one caveat to that is to monitor your own cravings. As I have mentioned there is a dopamine hit that comes with the chase on Apps. They are designed that way. Stay healthy in your screen time and the way you connect with others on screen. Never take things personally and you can always delete the ones that just aren't polite, courteous or attentive.

Remember that the individuals you connect with are just that. Individuals. One experience does not determine what the next will bring. Constant self-awareness and willingness to engage again can potentially bring you so much joy!

If you find yourself attracting a 'type', and you wish to move past that, I genuinely ask you to consider the psychology of, the subconscious patterns behind your choices. You may wish to engage with counselling, metaphysical healing or studies to help you understand yourself better. When we understand we can show ourselves more compassion and the result is a healthier relationship with ourselves. We may even grow to love ourselves and then truly healthy relationships come in to reflect that self-love back to us.

Meanwhile relationships are like a mirror. They help us see ourselves from different angles. Although this can sometimes be uncomfortable, it can also be rather Magickal, and eventually lead to creating something very special together.

Sometimes it involves being vulnerable to the things you worry about.

Are you subconsciously afraid of rejection?

Does he/she like me, does he/she not?

Am I looking perfect today?

The worst thing you can do is follow the shallow advice you see online to 'get your man/woman' or 'make him/her chase you'

These tactics have desperation written all over them and frankly they might get you a one-time result but they will drive you insane and make you over analyse yourself until there is nothing left of the real you to actually date because you will be thinking of the next tactic to make him like you. Seriously! As if there were never any successful relationships before the online advice!

He wants to know you!!! Not some fantasy you, that you have made up, because you think that is what he really wants!

So discover who you are. Explore your likes and dislikes so when he asks you, you aren't all tongue-tied.

Speak your mind, set your standards and say no when you need to.

Don't torture yourself with 'what if he leaves me?'

Value yourself.

Love yourself.

If you see yourself as valuable, he will too and if he doesn't get you as you are, he isn't the one, my love. He isn't the one.

Chapter 11
The Three Gregs. Greg Number 2

Greg number two was a gentleman from 'down the country' who came on with full-blown anger when we connected. 'You are too good to be real!' 'I bet your photos aren't like you at all'. 'Who wants world peace anyway?'

Ok, my profile may have sounded a little idealistic but actually that is a true representation of me! The majority of people who took the time to read it and to reply, loved it and would comment on the fact that it was rare to find someone authentic.

Obviously Greg number two was a little broken from previous experiences but it wasn't very endearing and if someone's first response to you is to criticise you online the wonderful thing is you can delete them!

AND I recommend you do! Promptly!

If you don't delete them, ask yourself why?

Are you out to 'rescue' this grown person, or is your self-worth so low that you see him as the relationship challenge you were looking for?

Just be honest with yourself and you won't be walking into something blindly.

In this instance I replied with, 'I'm genuinely sorry you feel this way. Perhaps you have had bad experiences on here before and that is colouring your response. **But this is me, and if I'm not your cup of tea that's ok. We can live and let live'.**

Then I deleted him.

Chapter 12
What's Love Got To Do With It?

Let's face it.

Ladies and gentlemen, we all desire romantic love, at some level. It's the fun part. But let's not get totally carried away with the highs and lows of those first flashes of passion!

If love is what you are after there are so many types of love described by the ancient Greeks, which are fun to explore.

Check which one you identify with the most and remember the consequences before you go there.

When you fall head over heels in infatuation and it doesn't work out, avoid going into victimhood and complaining, criticising and blaming. Women do have a tendency to do this. This is not cool and creates very low vibration energy on our beautiful planet.

Men are not our enemy. We are not their enemy.

The things we have ultimate control over are ourselves, our behaviour, and our responses to things that happen.

Each one of us is capable of making poor decisions.

Poor decisions can be based on many things including lack of self-respect, lack of self-love, or simple naivety.

We can learn and grow through experiences but take the time, to understand your motivations, and your desires. Take time to heal your wounds or, if you are not fully healed, be conscious of what it is that you bring to a new relationship.

I'd like to ask you a question. **'Would you date you?'**

If you are hesitating for one moment about the answer to this question, spend time lovingly reconnecting with the relationship you have with yourself.

Heal, Learn and Grow.

Remember life is a journey, and this is an ongoing adventure.

Ask yourself,

What is it that you want?

What do you desire?

In order to know the answer to these questions you really need to grow in your relationship with yourself first.

You need to get to know yourself.

This is a fundamental truth in life and interestingly, it is the decree written above the Gateway to all ancient Mystery Schools.

KNOW THYSELF!

Then, when we go into a relationship, and decisions need to be made, we come from a position of negotiation rather than falling in with the next plan that comes along and resenting it when you don't like it!

So let's explore the 7 types of love as described by the ancient Greek.

EROS

Passionate, physical desire! It starts quickly, burns brightly and can disappear just as quickly.

If you are set on experiencing this be aware that it may not last unless you are both willing to take the connection to another level.

PHILIA

This is the love between friends. It encompasses respect, honesty, trustworthiness, acceptance and good communication. This is the love that can build empires! A big part of this is loyalty.

♡ Once Upon A Tinder ♡

Is the person you hope to date in a phase of their dating life, where they are mesmerized by the selection of opportunities open to them? If so, are they always looking over their shoulder for the next beauty? Do they have a hard time being present with you? Is the grass always greener?

LUDUS

This embodies dating Apps a lot! It's the fun loving; laughter and dancing that come with a fleeting romance. There is, of course, nothing wrong with meeting lots of suitors. It's important to know what you really want in someone and that can take a little time to figure out, especially if you are going back on the dating scene after a long period of absence.

I will ask you to be honest with yourself. Are you ready?

In my first few encounters it was challenging to see past my fears of rejection and when you have been hurt please remember to avoid projecting those hurts on to any unsuspecting suitor. **It is important to have fun and to know how far you want to take intimacy. If like I did, you really want to go for it, remember to choose who you want to be close to carefully. You must take really good care of your body, your psychology and your soul during all of this.**

PRAGMA

This is literally likened to the opposite of 'falling' in love, which happens more easily. It is making a conscious choice to 'stand' in love with someone as a couple. This is something that generally develops over time and leads to true commitment to each other. It may include starting a family together, entwining finances together, turning up for each other in a much more committed way. This means to weather the storms of life together.

AGAPE

This is unselfish love. It is the purest expression of love, asking for nothing in return. It can encompass care for the world at large and combines it with action. The world needs this type of love.

PHILAUTIA

This is love of self.

It can be expressed in both a positive and negative way.

When negative we can become obsessed with fame, wealth or narcissism where we have an excessive need for attention or admiration, combined with a lack of empathy for others.

When expressed positively, self-love is healthy. We see our own need for growth, for good self-care and we respect our need for expression. It is fair to say we have to explore the question 'who am I?' to truly love ourselves and to ensure we nurture that need for self-love in a long lasting and healthy way.

STORGE

Unwavering devotion. This is the natural, instinctual, love of a parent for a child. It is willing to sacrifice oneself and to forgive even when wronged.

You may have been lucky enough to have already experienced each type of love.

Isn't life wonderful at helping us to have experiences that push us to grow and evolve? Whatever you are looking for, be clear, so you know what outcomes to expect.

When I was with my Italian lover, we knew that we had limited time together. There was no room for co-dependency or jealousy or neediness.

We used our time together in a very specific way, which demanded great communication, and this was so healing for me, it was exactly what I needed in order to trust men again and to trust my own judgement around men. I had to be willing to go there, and I found a good man.

He was young, but mature and oh so loving.

Chapter 13
The Three Gregs. Greg Number 3

*G*reg number three was a doctor on a round-the-world Clipper Race that had called into our city. We connected on Bumble on the day of his arrival. When one of these Clipper races arrives, the crew are welcomed with so much hospitality. It's a huge boost for the City in terms of a festival atmosphere with all the entertainment and spending associated with it.

He wasn't really interested in all of that. He was extremely fit, and the person who was sent up the mast on a regular basis to do whatever they do up the mast. He stayed on the boat while everyone went off drinking.

On day number two of their stay he asked me out to dinner. He was so sweet. There are only a limited number of clothes that you can bring on a trip like that. He was self conscious in what he was wearing. 'Normally I would dress up for such an occasion', he said. He was just a little taller than me and very affectionate.

We hit it off right away talking of medical stories and his experiences on the Clipper to date. He was in his mid 30's and had a wealth of experience working in Emergency Medicine. Thankfully he hadn't experienced too many emergencies on this longest leg of the race around the world. His plans were to return to his training in England when the race was complete. His family were based in Norway but he had come to the UK to train.

He spoke multiple languages and was very chivalrous. He wanted to know the best restaurant locally. I asked him what he liked to eat. He liked Italian or Indian food. We walked to the local Indian restaurant, which happened to have an Italian section on the menu.

He asked what was good and we ordered my favourites. We both shared a vegetarian Indian meal. His company was delightful and he was so polite.

It was obvious we liked each other, and I had never done the one-night-stand thing before. However this was the one and only night we had before his Clipper set sail the following afternoon. So when he asked me what I would like to do we discussed the possibilities.

He came home with me that night. We had tea and chatted some more. He was a complete gentleman and checked with me every step of the way if I thought this was a good idea or whether I would like to do this or that. He checked with me first without presuming anything down to the very first kiss.

When we finally went to bed my instincts were that I didn't want to have penetrative sex. I explained this to him and he honoured my wishes every step of the way. We did, however, experience a beautiful night of closeness where we kissed and touched and caressed and eventually climaxed together in a very connected way.

In today's world with so much on the menu in terms of sexual exploration, it is ultimately up to you, to know what feels like natural progression, and to find the words to COMMUNICATE that clearly. If something is not right COMMUNICATE that too.

Listen, respect and honour yourself AND the person you are with, whether it is a brief encounter, or whether it is in a longer-term relationship.

Consent is of utmost importance and NEVER be tempted to be in any way intimate with someone who is not in a position to give CLEAR consent.

The obvious example is when someone is heavily

under the influence of alcohol or drugs. It's impossible for them to be clear minded. Unfortunately, often alcohol or drugs are taken to help someone feel relaxed enough, to let their guard down long enough, to have the bravery it takes to get naked.

This leaves everything open to great misinterpretation. This is a heavy topic but an important one. Look out for yourself and each other. Care enough to make space for healing and compassion in all circumstances and be both responsible and kind.

If you find it difficult to find the words, or to relax and be present to your partner sexually, and you really wish this to be part of your life, start a conversation together and seek the help you need. I talk a lot about the fun side in this short book, but I am aware that we all carry wounds, hurts and blockages.

Some wounds are physical, some are psychological, some are emotional, some are sexual and some are spiritual. You deserve to heal and you deserve to find a great partner.

Remember your healing is down to you first. Make it so. You are your own responsibility.

When it comes to sex in a relationship, some days things will be all guns a blazing and other days the things of every day life will be a priority. Considering the worries about bills, the children, exams, the workload, it's a wonder there is time for intimacy at all in people's lives.

But, on the other hand sex can be an amazing stress reliever and a beautiful statement of connection between a couple.

It is an act of love, of creation, of devotion and of the bonding of opposites. It's power goes way beyond what we are taught to believe.

Actively creating time together can literally be the greatest gift you give each other.

After a hearty breakfast the next morning I left Greg (number 3) back to the Clipper. It was obvious our paths would not meet again but we appreciated the time together and that was enough.

He taught me so much in that short connection about the true meaning of being completely present to someone and their consensual needs. The impact was long lasting.

We said goodbye to each other on the pier and never communicated again.

Chapter 14
Love, Lust and Everything In Between

It takes time to build something special. Don't be in a hurry.

Having a lot of life experience can make you want to rush to a 'comfortable' place but each connection, each potential relationship is new, unique and worth forging.

Start with the premise that you are there to have fun.

Allow the gentleman to take the lead.

Remember I am speaking from my experience.

Your expression of femininity may be different, but if like me, you are attracted to very masculine men, let him prove himself to you.

As a woman entering the dating field, never invest more than you are receiving. It is your job to receive.

Don't mother your date in the beginning. Give him the opportunity to spoil you.

Value yourself as the prize he needs to win!

You be the judge as to whether he measures up.

Give him the opportunity to impress you.

This is a meeting of two people.

Get to know each other!

The first date is an exciting time!!

DON'T blow it by:

complaining,

being endlessly negative,

checking your phone constantly,

or pouring your heart out about how all men are losers (which they most certainly are NOT!)

or, because things are going well, planning how the marriage day might look!

DO:

Be playful.

Smile.

Flirt.

Listen actively to him and respond to his line of conversation,

Have interesting questions of your own but be careful not to interrogate especially on that first meeting.

Have fun!!!!!!

If you like him let him know, but make sure you end the evening, allowing him the chance to long for you.

If he isn't responding with adoration in the beginning he's not that into you. That's ok. Move on.

Of course, if you do not hear from him again….

Rejection is NOT a measure of your SELF WORTH!

If it doesn't end up on a second date don't replay over and over in your head.

There are an endless number of reasons why it didn't progress.

It just means that you found out sooner rather than later, that this is not 'the one'.

Stop wasting time analysing, while there are other good guys out there looking for love.

Dust yourself down and get back out there!!!

Be brave.

You are worth the effort and ultimately so is THE ONE!!!

You may be longing for intimacy.

It might have been a while, just remember, unless you are happy with a 'one nighter', take a little longer to get to know the person you are planning to get really naked with. You are your number one concern.

You are your guardian, your protector emotionally, spiritually and physically!

Don't forget to think contraception and safe sex!!!

Be kind to yourself and time will tell.

Be patient.

You will thank yourself!!!

Chapter 15
Changes

As time goes on you will want to change your profile and try something new. Initially I had photos only. I picked shots of my face up close, big smile. Then I added one of me sitting sipping tea where you could see the top half of my body. Then I had a full-length photo and finally, a group photo with friends.

On and off I would include a photo of me dancing (Pole fitness). That got variable responses from 'I love to dance too', to wolf whistles so it depended on how I felt as to whether I put those up.

When it came to my bio I had no idea how much information to give and certainly, initially, I didn't trust men or the dating App process so I was shy about putting anything up at all.

I left it blank in the beginning. It led to a lot of

inquiries about who I was, where I came from and what I did for a living.

I realised in the end, it was easier to write something. So, I put up the truth.

Don't lie. It's better someone is connecting because of who you are, not some fantasy version of you.

I posted what I do for a living. I said that I meditate. I said that I was vegetarian because I love animals. I stated that I didn't drink or smoke. I liked to keep fit and I travel a lot for my work. I stated that I am very independent. Friends said I shouldn't say I am independent as it suggests that I don't want to be won over by a man but it never seemed to cause me any problems. So I suggest you write a bio and run it by your friends (male and female) and see what they have to say. Then say what you personally like and give it a go! Test the responses. Saying something funny can be a great opener and help break the ice.

Just be you.

Other people's profiles vary widely too. Some literally write a book's worth. I find that a bit like laying all your cards on the table at once. You want to be able to start the conversation, but you don't want to give everything away. You want to have something to talk about if you meet. So write a few sentences stating a few interesting facts that invite more questions and see where it takes you. Maybe you will find yourself in the arms of someone you really like and who really likes you back.

Remember, everything great in life is worth waiting for. Rome wasn't built in a day. So don't rush meeting someone if it doesn't feel right.

On the other hand don't string each other on forever or the dazzle will fizzle out.

I have a friend who does polite introductions then asks if you are interested in meeting for a coffee. He says it cuts down on endless texting when you really don't know if you like someone until you meet anyway.

There is a point to this. However if someone is asking me where I live, and whether I live alone in the first sentences I get a little 'creeped out' and cut off very soon.

Always put yourself in the shoes of the other person reading your communication. Simple words can change the whole dynamic very quickly. I would add that the energy you send out with the text is important too.

Don't text if you are in fowl form. It will be felt on the other side. We are energetic beings, quantum physics tells us this, and feelings travel.

Always remember this is someone new. It is not the guy who 'dumped you' last month.

Give this new person a chance and don't project your previous experiences or fears on to this unsuspecting free spirit!

If necessary, get counselling and/or study Metaphysics. Work on yourself.

Be the best version of yourself for you first.

After all you have to live with you, in your own head!

Then, do it for the person you love.

Chapter 16
The Widower

I met a truly delightful man on Tinder who was starting to date again after the death of his wife. She had passed away almost 7 years previously so I felt it would be ok.

Dating a widower is a whole other experience and you will have to have a very strong personal identity. I also advise that you take potential challenges into consideration.

There is something that happens to a human being when they lose the love of their life to death. Firstly they naturally put their loved one on a pedestal.

Be prepared to see photos of them everywhere especially (and naturally) if they had children together.

Of course it depends on their relationship but it's possible that you will never fully measure up. You may have to play 'second fiddle' to their now dead beloved. The first year after the loss is particularly difficult. There are so many milestones including first birthday, first anniversary, first Christmas and you will need to be particularly sensitive to each of these events.

However, the fact that someone is willing to start again is a huge compliment to you. Remember to be open to talking about things that draw you into their previous life and you will need to have an appreciation of the way things were before you came on the scene.

At the same time, there has to be a healthy balance in creating something new for both of you. It's ok to admit that maybe it's a little too much for you at times.

You are not their counsellor but relationship building does require being there for someone in the good and the hard times. Just be mindful of your own self-care.

My widower's father was ailing at the time we met. He was a very caring person but, as time went on it became apparent, he was not ready to date. His grief was being highlighted again, by the grief being brought up by the pending death of his father.

Our dates from the start involved discussions regarding treatments and caring.

One day my widower was so low he told me he

♡ Once Upon A Tinder ♡

felt suicidal. At that moment I was completely frozen in terror at the idea that he may actually do this. He was away on a break in England and there was no way I could be with him. We were communicating by phone. After giving all the advice I could and talking into the small hours, he slept. When I called him the following day he had no recollection of having said it to me. He may have been drinking at the time. We were three months into the developing relationship. At that point, I had to pull out as that was too much for me to carry. I told him I couldn't continue and we split up.

I have never regretted that parting. His father lived a good quality life for another 9 months. I visited his father a week before he died to say my goodbyes. He was a lovely elderly gentleman. The dear widower was doing well and I knew in my heart that he would be ok. I also knew he still had work to do on himself. I wished him well and left. We never spoke again.

This is a particularly heavy scenario but very real. Don't be under any illusions. Get to know a person before you grow into a relationship that has many entanglements. As we each grow older we have our stuff but that means we should be constantly willing to work on ourselves and grow. You are your number one priority.

You are not here to fix, mend or 'save' anyone else.

That is their job. And you are your job.

Of course you can offer advice and comfort and be present but be aware that if someone cannot see their part to play, or they are either unwilling or unready to heal, don't encourage that stagnancy by staying beyond what is fair to you.

Observe the type of person you attract.

Is it always someone who needs rescuing? There are plenty of well-rounded mature individuals out there to date. We all have our scars and each of us has a personal responsibility to work on them.

Set your standards high and be an example of high standards.

Remember that.

Chapter 17
Mindset

Don't let one, two or more 'bad' dates get you down.

Situations don't always turn out the way we wished.

It's a bit like a training ground.

Each connection is a test.

We will receive the same test over and over until we learn the lesson!

How you conduct yourself will determine the calibre of the next test.

You will of course experience treats along the way!

Those treats keep giving us the courage to come back for another taste!

There is something really worth being aware of.

If you have lost a love due to infidelity it can make you suspicious of new relationships, yes.

As I have said before, where possible, monitor your thoughts and do not project that on to a new connection.

However, there is more to this point. It can also make you suspicious of other Goddesses.

THE BATTLE BETWEEN WOMEN NEEDS TO END!!!

Our sisters are our sisters! If a guy wants to date you while he is still with another Goddess, what does that say about him?

And, while you may be tempted, if you consider dating him, what does that say about you?

Compassionately, ask yourself why you are so desperate to have a man in your life that you would consider being with someone who is already romantically involved with someone else, while that someone else has no idea that their man is considering 'cheating' on them.

Don't be passive in your decision-making.

Call the other person out to help them see themselves and be the catalyst to help them to grow up!

Adult relationships require full responsibility for our actions.

Being a part of infidelity invites messiness into your life, and you are setting yourself up for heartache. You are cheating on another Goddess while you are with someone who is willing to do this to the Goddess in his life!

Let him sort out his relationship, his life, his issues, his mess.

Value your time, your emotional and psychological health and be kind to other people.

No one is perfect but there are standards and you really want to hold true to those for yourself.

If common decency doesn't motivate you to be a good person then simply remember that karma is rarely forgiving!

So what is it that you need to focus on while waiting for Mr. Right?

Healthy Body: Clean up your nutrition and gut health, exercise regularly including cardio, muscle mass and flexibility, use supplements where necessary, and protect your immunity. Are you actively doing things that decrease your immunity: poor sleep, excess sugar, alcohol or smoking?

Healthy Mind: Are you letting your thoughts think the worst of yourself or others? According to Metaphysics we can actively make life worse for ourselves by consistently expecting the worst. Consider metaphysical studies to actively create a better life.

Spirit: Everyone has an essential spark that flows through them, bringing energy, joy and passion! Your expression of that will be unique to you. Cultivate this so everything you touch receives your unique fire inside!

Wealth: Have you mastered your finances? If not, take an honest look at it and take control. Seek advice if you need to. Independence when you get to the relationship of your dreams is important. Shared expenses may come further down the line but ensuring you each have your own account will guarantee that you can buy the silly stuff the other won't fully understand and you can surprise each other when you need to. This will help you both maintain essential independence.

Relationships: Family, friends and colleagues. The COVID-19 experience has meant our connections have been more distant than usual but staying connected whether in a relationship or not is essential to the fabric of living. Whether you are shy, uncomfortable in company or whether you are the party planner, maintain your relationships and take care of your loved ones. Loving is one of the greatest pleasures in life and if you are lucky enough to receive it in return lavish in it! We only have one life!!!

Joy: What fills you up? What helps you get out of bed in the morning? What makes you smile, laugh and dance? What gives you tingles?

It's different for everyone but this is really important to make time for. Make a list and promise yourself regular doses of your joy! It might be an online class in your favourite dance. If you aren't sure, explore. This is one of the ingredients to a fulfilling life.

Be in a position where a new relationship isn't there to fix you, it's there to add to your already amazing, fulfilling life!

Be happy with you first!

Chapter 18
The Rock Star

As I sat swiping one day I came across one of the most beautiful men I have ever seen. He reminded me of an era in my life when I first felt attracted to men. He had long hair, a laid-back stance, dreamy eyes and a fabulous dress sense. I swiped right not expecting to hear from him as our backgrounds were quite different, but we actually matched.

It was Tinder, and I didn't start the conversation. I waited until he said hi, which was a number of weeks later.

Never feel in a rush. Let him come to you. If the timing is right and he is authentically interested he will step up.

I have a life that I love. A gentleman will either step up or he won't. Either way, I get on with living my own life! I don't push anything before its time.

Then if nothing is progressing, despite my making it fairly obvious that I like him, (I had swiped right), I happily move on. I like a man to know what he likes and to go after it.

We chatted back and forth for a while.

He asked to meet. I chose a public, neutral zone and we met in the Botanical gardens in Belfast. He was immediately identifiable from his photos. Again, I cannot emphasise how incredibly handsome he was. He had tied his hair back in a ponytail. He had a fashionable hat on his head and a short well groomed beard. He was tall and slender, at least a full head height taller than me, and he wore denim jeans and jacket. He wore a fabulous T-shirt and he had an interesting Belfast accent.

We walked around the grounds. He was a fast walker and for some reason I had chosen heeled boots so I had to ask him to slow down.

He is a member of a world-recognised band. He played guitar and travelled a lot. We walked in the rose garden, which was in full bloom. I stopped to smell the roses at different points and it really was a rather intoxicating experience. He was the exact same age as me and like me, he felt a lot younger.

He took great pride in his fitness levels and it was obvious he was fit.

He was one of seven kids, all adopted. His original parents were from Malaysia and Portugal. They had met as medical students in Belfast. He never felt the urge to find them. He was particularly close to his adoptive mum and he spoke about her in glowing terms. I liked his respect for her. He asked me to join him for dinner. Restaurants were just beginning to open again after a period of closure due to COVID-19. We found a spot and I noticed how he treated our waitress. He was conversational, approachable, funny and paid for everything. He was very gentlemanly. The conversation flowed easily. We laughed at the same things.

Turns out he had studied music in London while I studied medicine in Belfast. I had this incredible feeling that if we had met earlier in our lives we may have married and had kids but that was probably just a fantasy. It did feel real somehow.

It got late, and a decision had to be made. Was I going to stay or return home (an hour and a half drive away). I decided to return home. It felt like the right thing.

After that meeting, he called me daily. He told me he was disappointed I hadn't stayed. I guess that was a good sign that he wanted to see me again.

His family had a home near the seaside and it so happened, that on my birthday weekend, he would be there alone. He invited me to stay. I was really excited BUT I also felt anxious. He was crazy handsome and somehow that unnerved me.

On my arrival he had been working on his road bike and appeared relaxed but he was really attentive and wanted to know if I needed anything to drink. I had a cup of tea. We talked and laughed. It was getting late.

He showed me around the entirety of the house and lastly, the room we both could sleep in, if that's what I wanted. I was good with that. He carried my bag in from the car. I got ready for bed in the bathroom and when I returned in my little nightdress I felt really self conscious and started to ask silly questions like, is this what he really wanted?

He smiled and reassured me. I climbed under the covers and he pulled me close to his warm body. We kissed. I melted.

Our last kiss had been on the cheek in Belfast weeks previously, but it felt as if we knew each other really well. We had talked daily since then.

His presence was so calm and we played with each other's hair. We never stopped smiling at each other.

Our chemistry was quite something.

I actually counted the number of times we had 'coitus' that night. FIVE times! It felt as if we could have lived in that bed, a bit like those photos of John Lennon and Yoko Ono.

This was one of those nuclear moments in time, which fuels you for many recollections. It has certainly added fuel to my fire on many occasions since!

That weekend, we spent time walking together and just being in each other's company. It was very surreal. The beach was just a stroll away. We laughed at the same things and shared a love of Science Fiction.

I had spent a lot of time playing on those beaches as a child.

He liked being outdoors, so did I.

I showed him some beaches he hadn't been to before.

I really liked his company.

Afterwards, we stayed in touch daily and we met up regularly during the summer months.

Unfortunately, that was it.

A summer romance.

Ten weeks after we first connected, he didn't respond to a text. I called and there was no answer. Eventually he responded by text to say he was with his brother and would contact me after the weekend.

He never called.

I guess that is what they call 'ghosting'.

It's what someone does when they are no longer interested and don't want the discomfort of an honest conversation. It really means they are not ready for, or interested in, a responsible, grown up relationship with you.

It was the first time anything like that had ever happened to me.

It hurt at the time but, as I said, I'm most definitely not someone who pursues.

If this happens to you, don't fall into the trap of 'maybe'.

Maybe, he is still interested, maybe something happened to him or maybe I should call?

'Maybe' under these circumstances unfortunately means 'no'.

Interestingly, around that time, I started to connect with someone very special at my workplace.

I don't know if it was fate, but the Rock Star romance faded as quickly as it started. All I can say is, that with my heart, I genuinely wish him all good things.

Our lifestyles wouldn't have been compatible longer term.

But, hey, a cheeky smile still spreads across my face when I think of him.

Chapter 19
Polarity Between The Sexes

Not everyone expresses their gender identity or their sexual preferences in the same way.

I am speaking as a heterosexual female using dating Apps.

In my experience, men and women are so different!

These differences can lead to heartache or true reason for celebration.

We have to acknowledge and explore the differences in order to navigate dating.

Some helpful hints as you get to know each other.

How are Men and Women different?

Men are focused, while women have a wider outlook. An example of this would be, if he isn't responding immediately to your message give him time to respond. He could well be working and intensely engaged in what he is doing.

Take back control of your mind. Remember that the inner critic has a tendency to criticise you AND others. Take back control and sense the divine in others first and foremost.

Exercise understanding and reasoning. And add a good dollop of discernment.

Occupy yourself with creating the life of your dreams. Don't give him a hard time for being busy doing his job. In relationship building and maintenance, there are fewer things more destructive than a woman who 'nags.' Please don't take that the wrong way, it's simply true.

The truth is that it feels terrible to be on the receiving end of constant criticism.

On the other hand, it can also be equally difficult when one's legitimate requests are being ignored.

Change is hard when both parties feel that the other one should change.

What to do? Take ownership of your feelings.

Make sure positive comments outweigh negative ones by a healthy margin.

No relationship will survive if a person feels more judged than admired.

So, take your inner monologue to task. Remember, even if you don't say anything the energy of those thoughts will seep through your texts, your messages and your connection to one another.

The answer to all of this is to **HEAL.**

Heal the conscious and the subconscious mind. If you are serious about being the best version of yourself, consider the **Path of The Initiate.** Check out my website! I have contacts all over the world who are more than willing to Guide you.

Also, remember you will require a degree of compatibility in your longer term plans if this relationship is to last. So as you get to know each other, talk about what you want for the future.

Are your plans compatible? Does he want children and you don't? Do you plan to live on opposite sides of the planet?

Don't leave your heartache or your joy to chance. Explore if there is a way to meet each other midway and if not, agree to part. Not every relationship is meant to last long term. **Heal, Learn and Grow**.

Of note, men are problem solvers, while women are emotion driven. This means that if you need someone to listen to your problems without solving them, phone your female friends.

However, a word of caution.

Many women have been taught that complaining, criticizing, and 'bitching' is a legitimate way to deal with problems. This is incorrect. It sends out very low vibration energy and actually creates havoc in our world.

In reality almost everything has to do with our relationship with ourselves first. Until we heal that as men and women, we generally create problems for ourselves.

Next, men are motivated by purpose, so make room for his vision in life. Women are more free flowing and adaptive but as a woman your vision is important too. You must actively create and engage with it. Otherwise resentment will follow. You must **'KNOW THYSELF'**.

Before you set foot in the dating world, figure out what it is that you desire for your life path. That way you have your own compass. Plans change but if you know yourself first, when you meet someone, you each have a vision.

Importantly, never go into a relationship thinking you will change the other person! That is the height of arrogance, even when it is well intentioned.

So when you finally connect, do you love spending time together, have you got good communication, are you respectful of each other, are you honest and loyal to each other? Do you have similar values? Do you think in the same way about finances? Do you feel the same way about having family?

Spend time discussing those visions so you can figure out together what works. That way you build together and move in harmony towards a future that is mutually joy filled.

In summary, do not project, do not criticise.

Do chill, do be you. Above all, be kind to yourself and to each other.

Chapter 20
Growing Bolder

With a few extra years of maturity, changes come to your body.

Being menopausal does not protect you against sexually transmitted diseases or pregnancy. Currently held medical beliefs suggest that you can still become pregnant up to 2 years after your last period.

Starting a sexual relationship with a new partner still requires safe sex.

Consider the use of condoms and explore your expectations with regards to monogamy.

A dip in libido after menopause is both normal and common. I have a delightful acupuncturist who looked at me with such pity because she knew how much I love sex. I have to say I am so grateful when I refused to believe her when she said my libido would not return when my periods stopped.

If there is a dip in your sex drive and it is important to you, my advice is, keep active!

It's like self-rediscovery with less oestrogen! Go on a safari for lube, moisturisers whatever it takes to keep you moist and use your vibrator if you are not in a sexual relationship.

With less oestrogen, the walls of the vagina may thin and become a little less elastic. Topical oestrogen works! Speak to your doctor.

The saying 'use it or lose it' comes to mind!

If you abstain for a very long time the vagina can atrophy slightly making reengagement with sexual activity painful.

Avoid this by maintaining sensual connection with yourself.

If to date, you have not, please do not fear, vaginal dilators are an option if necessary. But let's avoid them if we can.

This gives a new meaning to the importance of foreplay! Know what works for you and make sure it's something you discuss with your partner! They will be so pleased to be the source of your pleasure believe me!

Also bear in mind, if one position is not comfortable, try another! Be creative. Have fun!

Maintain your flexibility. Take up yoga!

Why is all of this important?

Because we rarely talk about these things!

Sex ought to be one of our greatest pleasures in life. I acknowledge this is not the case for so many and my heart goes out to those who have experienced physical, mental or sexual abuse. If what I write helps you to rediscover yourself again then I am grateful that you were brave enough to explore for yourself.

Please seek sensitive professional psychological help if this is needed.

Libido is difficult to measure and science finds it challenging to quantify.

While hormones play their part, physical, social and psychological influences play their role too.

In their twenties male testosterone is high, but anxiety can lead to erectile dysfunction in 8% overall.

Females are most fertile in their late teens to early twenties but generally have more sex drive in their late 20's when hormones change.

Men continue to have a strong sex drive throughout their 30's and 40's but other pressures like family, work and commitments can reduce their drive.

Testosterone generally starts to decrease by 1% per year from age 35 onwards.

Pregnancy has variable affects on sex drive.

Sometimes this is coupled with anxiety around potential effects on the baby. Always check with your doctor if you are unsure.

As men age their ability to have erections changes. Men and women both should enjoy a healthy sex life until they are much older. Problems that arise with aging include heart disease, diabetes and the drugs used to treat them. An honest conversation with your doctor will help hugely.

For men it is extremely important that you speak to your doctor about options for treating erectile dysfunction (ED).

For women over 50, weight gain, hot flushes, anxiety and sleep problems can lessen sex drive. Talk to your doctor about possible solutions.

And remember, it's not just about hormones, physical and mental wellbeing are also important.

Your health is your wealth.

Chapter 21
YOU, HIM, HER, THE ENTIRE UNIVERSE

We are all here on this tiny blue planet in this big flavoursome soup called life.

We each bring a different flavour to the pot and some are just not meant to go together no matter how hard you try.

It's ok.

There are over 7 billion people on this planet and we are more connected now than ever before, at least through technology, Apps, dating sites and social media!

Love can seem illusive in this bustling world but it is so worth the effort.

Perhaps you can appreciate that when we care for, nurture and love ourselves we aren't coming from a place of need.

Rather a place of contentment.
Not all relationships work out.
That's also ok.
Some are not meant to.

How you conduct your departure from your previous connection and how you engage with your onward journey are very much down to you.

It can be a time of trepidation but self-care and continued work on yourself will see you through with the support of friends and family.

Remember, the only real 'control' we have is over our responses, our behaviours and ourselves.

Self-awareness is a key to dealing with all issues in life.

If a particular situation is not going the way you hoped, ask yourself the following questions.

What is my part in this?
Where have I made it better?
Where have I made it worse?
What steps can I take that are wiser?
How will I change this pattern in my life?
What is possible?
What is not possible?

Answers to the above questions will differ from person to person.

That is why self-awareness and on-going work on self-worth, self-growth and spiritual wellbeing are important.

Take responsibility.

In reality almost everything has to do with our relationship with ourselves firstly and not others.

If you are not being treated the way you desire, work on yourself, communicate and if things don't change, why are you still in the relationship?

Until we heal these things in ourselves as men and women we keep creating problems for ourselves.

Your path will be different to the ones in this manual. Whether you choose to use or ignore any of the advice is up to you. Whatever you do, you will learn and I wish you every joy along the way!

Remember

Heal, Learn, Grow
Above All
Know Thyself!

Chapter 22
In Summary: Tips To Take Away

Chapter 1 How it all Started
Interestingly, from that moment forward any city I travelled to in the world, I made it one of my priorities to visit at least one sex shop and treat myself to a new toy.

Chapter 2 A Little Know How
'Swipe left if you don't want to meet them. Swipe right if you would consider meeting them'. In the beginning I swiped right a lot!

Chapter 3 My First Date
Timing on a date is important. I met an incredibly successful gentleman who taught me a lot about etiquette and how to communicate your affection through attention to detail.

Chapter 4 Self Care First

There may be days when you would do anything to feel the arms of a tall dark handsome stranger around you, however my lovely, YOU need to LOVE YOU FIRST.

Chapter 5 A Second Go

I was put on this planet to love men and maybe even inspire other women to do so too. The opposite sexes have spent way too long tearing each other down.

Chapter 6 Good Boundaries

If things are not working out, it's ok! STOP letting your thoughts eat you up inside. Instead, concentrate on creating the life of your dreams!

Chapter 7 A Surprise!

Interestingly, he just wanted to satisfy me. I was in ecstasy!

Chapter 8 The Chemistry Behind Falling For Someone

Sometimes the whole process of falling for someone can feel like you are going insane. There are good chemical reasons for this.

Our hearts flutter, our cheeks flush, and our palms may feel sweaty while emotionally we get mixed feelings of passion and nervousness.

Chapter 9 Greg Number 1
He had a very straight-laced profile but when we got talking he would send really naked pictures of his athletic body.

Chapter 10 Getting to know you, getting to know all about you.
If you see yourself as valuable, he will too and if he doesn't get you as you are, he isn't the one, my love. He isn't the one.

Chapter 11 Greg Number 2
But this is me, and if I'm not your cup of tea that's ok. We can live and let live.

Chapter 12 What's Love Got To Do With It?
Would you date you?

The things we have ultimate control over are ourselves, our behaviour and our responses to things that happen.

It is important to have fun and to know how far you want to take intimacy. If like I did, you really want to go for it, remember to choose who you want to be close to carefully. You must take really good care of your body, your psychology and your soul during all of this.

Chapter 13 Greg Number 3
In today's world with so much on the menu in terms of sexual exploration it is ultimately up to you to know what feels like a natural progression and to find the words to COMMUNICATE that clearly. If something is not right COMMUNICATE that too.

Chapter 14 Love, Lust and Everything In Between
Rejection is NOT a measure of your SELF WORTH!

You are your guardian, your protector emotionally, spiritually and physically!

Don't forget to think contraception and safe sex!!!

Chapter 15 Changes
Be the best version of yourself for you first.

After all you have to live with you, in your own head!

Then, do it for the person you love.

Chapter 16 The Widower
Set your standards high and be an example of high standards.

Chapter 17 Mindset
THE BATTLE BETWEEN WOMEN NEEDS TO END!!!

Adult relationships require full responsibility for our actions.

Be in a position where a new relationship isn't there to fix you, it's there to add to your already amazing, fulfilling life! Be happy with you first!

Chapter 18 The Rock Star
Our lifestyles wouldn't have been compatible longer term.

But, hey, a cheeky smile still spreads across my face when I think of him.

Chapter 19 Polarity between the Sexes
Exercise understanding and reasoning. And add a good dollop of discernment.

No relationship will survive if a person feels more judged than admired.

In summary, do not project, do not criticise.

Do chill, do be you.

Above all, be kind to yourself and to each other.

Chapter 20 Growing Bolder
Libido is difficult to measure and science finds it challenging to quantify.

If there is a dip in your sex drive and it is important to you, my advice is, keep active!

Your health is your wealth.

Chapter 21 YOU, HIM, HER, THE ENTIRE UNIVERSE

>Heal, Learn, Grow
>Above All
>Know Thyself!

Thank you for taking the time to
read this book. I hope you enjoyed it and that it
assists you on your journey to finding love.
With my love, Dr Ann ♡

Acknowledgements and Gratitude

In the beginning my parents, whom I adore, taught me my first observations regarding the differences between men and women. After fifty-seven years they are still lovingly together and I admire their honest tenacity and wonderful courage. I love you both with all of my heart and thank you for all the sacrifices and on-going guidance, which have helped me to become the woman I am today.

To my two brothers Martin and Cahal. We played Cowboys and Indians together, built dens in hedges and fought like cats and dogs. We learned so much together and now we have each other's backs in this world. Thank you for being the wonderful men you are.

To my beautiful and loving sister-in-law

Fionnuala. A kinder soul you could not meet. A genuine Angel on this earth.

To my Godson Charlie. I'm so proud of you! And my darling niece Nadia. You remind me so much of me. To my Goddaughter Clare, a little Star radiant with song and dance.

To all my cousins, who taught me so much. I loved listening to your stories about boyfriends and girlfriends. I was one of the youngest and probably the least cool but you tolerated me tagging along to those roller discos!

To my aunts and uncles who drove us to and from the late night entertainments. Bless your patience and your kindness during those teenage doldrums.

To my friends in particular; Siobhan McCusker. We never left each other's side throughout primary school. Liza Brogan, talented artist, who now sings to us from Heaven. Anne and Mark Gooding, Pauline McAlinney, Sheila Smart, little Fiona Quinn, tall Fiona Quinn, Shirley Foreshaw, Siobhan Carey, Siobhan Donaghy, Anna Zschocke, Helen Burke and all your beloveds and all my fellow classmates in college! You honoured me greatly by sharing some of my most formative moments. Rose Reel, you taught me my first introductions to energy medicine and listened to me when I needed it most.

Thank you all!

♡ Once Upon A Tinder ♡

To all the boyfriends before I got married, the brief encounters and the longer courtships. Each one was precious to me. I hope you each found the love you deserve.

To my ex-husband, a genuinely good soul, who has found love again. I am genuinely happy for you. To all your loving family whom I miss, and respectfully give space to, so life can move on in the way it is meant to, thank you for the precious moments gathered in knowing you.

To every colleague, in every role, whom I have had the privilege to work with, in general practice, hospital and hospice, you are each a shining star. Thank you for your kindness to me and your service to all.

To all the patients I have had the privilege of caring for, all clients who trust me with their precious journeys in life and all students who are willing to learn, bless you, in every facet of life. May you know true JOY, in all its colourful arrays.

To my own mentors and teachers from Primary school, to Grammar school, to Medical School and to Mystery school. I have had the privilege of learning from the best.

In particular I would like to thank three of the bravest men I know, who fight daily for peace on this planet. Founder Gudni Gudnason, Ipsissimus Dave

Lanyon and Ipsissimus Hideto Nakagome. Each has and continues to inspire me to greater heights of understanding of the Magick in this life with its infinite possibilities. Because of their patience and sacred teaching I love my life and continue to encourage others to do the same. The Modern Mystery School is open to all who seek to know more.

To the Women of the Counsel of Twelve with whom I have the privilege of serving, your unique gifts inspire me daily and I rejoice in knowing each of you. In the west, Divina Franca Lanyon, Divina Liza Rossi, Divina Theresa Bullard, Divina Rita Van Den Berg, Divina Kate Bartram Brown, and in the east Divina Eiko Gudnason, Divina Louisa Nakagome, Divina Tsukiko Kimura, Divina Maki Otani, Divina Suzuki Kitamura, Divina Yoda Asuza.

To the Leader of Leaders Eric Thompson, warrior of peace and true gentleman.

To the ever wise, ever youthful Western World Oracle dear Verla Wade.

To my dear friend & confidant whom I admire with all my heart, Sandra Raid. Thank you for the honour of your company in this wondrous life.

To my beautiful Guide Martina Coogan, without whom, I would never have discovered the Mystery School or walked the Path therein. Thank you!

To the countless men and women across the globe, who share the Mystery School Path with me. I admire your courage in keeping your heart open in a world that often seeks to shut it. Remember the Magick and your sacred tools when you most need them!

To my wonderful mentors who introduced me to the possibilities of putting these ideas in print. Mirav Tarkka my coach, Heidi De Love my meticulous proof reader and Parul Agrawal my publishing mentor, bless each of you amid the powerful work you do!

And of course, to my lovers. You inspired me always, no matter how it started, how it ended, whatever in between. I honour you, dear men in my life. You enriched my life with your uniqueness. Thank you, with all my heart.

To all men and all women, we are figuring life out every day. By now you probably realise that relationships are both a nurturing space and a training ground.

May we all learn to love one another again and bring peace to our broken hearts, our broken relationships and our broken world.

May each of us dare to love full-heartedly!!!

About the Author

Dr Ann Donnelly
MB MRCGP DRCOG DFP DYT Dippallmed Lfhom

Dr Ann graduated from Queen's University Belfast in Medicine in 1992. She is a member of the Royal College of General Practitioners. She holds Diplomas in Obstetrics and Gynaecology, in Family Planning, in Palliative Medicine and in Yoga Teaching. She has studied with the British Medical Acupuncture Society and the Faculty of Homeopathy. She is a NLP practitioner and an Emotional Freedom Therapy Advocate. She is a Facilitator for Advanced Communication Skills for health care professionals. She has been instrumental in helping to develop a Foundation Degree in Holistic and Integrative Therapies.

She is often consulted as a medical expert in the media including Yahoo, Cosmopolitan and Glamour.

Dr Ann began her studies in Metaphysics with the Modern Mystery School in 2006. She has graduated as a Life Activation Practitioner, a Healer and Guide. She is also an Ensofic Ray Practitioner and a Fundamental Ensofic Reiki Teacher. Her studies have developed her understanding of the importance of ceremony in healing and to this end she is an Egyptian Priestess and a Wiccan Priestess both in the Lineage of King Salomon. She is an International Teacher with the Modern Mystery School while continuing her studies as an Apprentice Universal Hermetic Ray Kabbalah Teacher.

Divina Ann also serves as a Member of the Counsel of 12 women.

To connect please email:
thelovedoctor@onceuponatinder.com
Website: onceuponatinder.com